You and Tarot

HOW TO READ THE CARDS

Bryan Cavan Doyle

 FriesenPress

One Printers Way
Altona, MB R0G 0B0
Canada

www.friesenpress.com

The author acknowledges the splendid work by Kelena Lee supporting *You and Tarot* in the area of computer expertise and her patience in dealing with the writer and his lack of I.T acumen.

ISBN
978-1-03-910940-7 (Hardcover)
978-1-03-910939-1 (Paperback)
978-1-03-910941-4 (eBook)

1. *Body, Mind & Spirit, Divination, Tarot*

Distributed to the trade by The Ingram Book Company

THIS BOOK IS DEDICATED TO ALL SEEKERS
OF TRUTH AND HEALING.

Table of Contents

Introduction

Do not say "I have found the truth," say "I have found a truth."
— Khalil Gibran

Your intuitive energy is neutral; it is your mind that creates a positive or negative interpretation of the state of affairs. When it rains when you have planned a picnic, you may say the weather is bad; however, if you are a keen gardener, you may say that it is good. In fact, it is just weather. For some, reading tarot cards is light entertainment; for others, it is a tool that can be used to uncover information and, at the same time, reveal truth and healing to the seeker. Tarot is capable of illuminating profound insights, which bring clarity and lucidity for the reader and the querent. People who ask to have their cards read are looking for answers that will help solve the quandary they find themselves in.

Nothing happens until something moves.
— Albert Einstein

Tarot readings are not passive experiences that give you peace of mind whilst you continue living your life as before the reading. If you do find yourself in this state, then nothing will change, you will continue to be a victim of circumstances. You have the responsibility to initiate the required change. Whether the change is physical, mental, or psychological, it is up to you to act, to bring about the required truth and healing that will increase your well-being in all aspects of your being. If you decide to do nothing, then you will continue to go through this period of your life "pulling" on "push" doors. On the other hand, when you decide to make even the smallest change in your thought processes or habits, the world will embrace you and fresh opportunities will guide you from the dark path to the right road of existence.

I will abandon everything I have outgrown.
— Wallace D. Wattles

Life is a learning curve. Mistakes can be forgiven, but not forgotten. Your spiritual growth demands that any past or current habits impeding your way to a better life be left behind in your trash can of bad choices. It is time to move onward. Your courage is needed to propel you to a better life.

The Tarot Card Deck

The deck contains seventy-eight cards. Twenty-two cards are under the title of Major Arcana. The meaning of "arcana" is secret, or hidden. The remaining fifty-six cards are known as Minor Arcana, or Lesser Arcana. The secret or mystery can be revealed within the tarot reading through the intuition of the reader coupled with the energies of both reader and seeker. Adding the twenty-two Major cards and the fifty-six Minor cards brings the deck to a grand total of seventy-eight.

Tarot Major Arcana Cards

0.	The Fool	11.	Justice
1.	The Magician	12.	The Hanged Man
2.	The High Priestess	13.	Death
3.	The Empress	14.	Temperance
4.	The Emperor	15.	The Devil
5.	The Hierophant	16.	The Tower
6.	The Lovers	17.	The Star
7.	The Chariot	18.	The Moon
8.	Strength	19.	The Sun
9.	The Hermit	20.	Judgment
10.	Wheel of Fortune	21.	The World

Total of 22 Tarot Major Arcana Cards

The Fool is certainly dressed for a celebration as opposed to leaping from a cliff. With his white dog and white rose, these symbols of pet projects and new beginnings emphasize the meaning of the scenario, which is the starting of something completely new, the birth of an idea or an ideal, something that the heart of the seeker yearns for. In addition, white is the energy of purity and lucidity. It is not uncommon for the seeker to have no experience of the venture they are willing to explore; whether it is successful or not, it is a grand learning curve that will always lead to something better. Curiosity is the key that leads to putting aside time for this idyllic adventure. If the enquirer is waiting for the perfect time and opportunity to begin this pursuit, it will probably never happen. Tarot created this story to show the seeker the time is now: Start from the very beginning and see where the journey takes you. All indications are you will be a better person because of your individual initiative.

THE MAGICIAN.

The Magician emits energies that are sometimes inexplicable, and it is all through the beauty of truth: All his cards are on the table—pentacles, swords, wands, and cups. Crowning his head is the symbol of eternity, sometimes known as the symbol of infinity. His left hand holds the sceptre of royal assent, as the other hand points downwards, indicating "as above so below," as in the Lord's Prayer, "on earth, as it is in heaven." Nature's abundance is growing throughout the scene, showing the way for natural progression for whatever is on the mind of the seeker. The magician is wearing red for action, and white for purity, protection, and truth. Part of the message is to be honest with yourself, as well as with all others who are involved. Being a magician also means that one does not give away the secret of the act: Be cautious, a letter of disclosure may be something to consider if it is a business venture. Magic and logic are siblings in many transactions. The tabletop is orange, the energy of change, and, in this case, it is change for the better. Anything that looks magical has hard work and practice behind it.

THE HIGH PRIESTESS

The High Priestess is a card of emotions, intuition, and creativity. She sits between the pillars of positive and negative, symbolizing balance. Her crown, with the moon prominently placed, rules the seeker's moods as they ebb and flow. Three of the major religions are represented, with the Cross, the Torah, and the Crescent, some of the roads leading to Heaven. Earth's abundance in full bloom around the throne emulates the promise of a fruitful future. When a seeker draws this card, it represents a green light to go forward with their wishes—and reminds one to keep a careful eye upon the positive and negative energies, not only of the self, but also all participants involved in the venture, whether it be personal, financial, or spiritual. The religious aspect of the card is a reminder to honour all beliefs of all who are involved. Take note of the columns. They are not black and white; they are black and grey, which indicates compromise. The priestess is gowned mostly in blue, the energy of teaching, learning, and calmness, with the white energy flowing throughout the folds for truth, lucidity, and protection. Because it is a high court card, patience is one of the virtues that should be observed.

The Empress is the softer side of the seeker's personality. She is well cushioned upon her seat of authority, waiting to hear from the enquirer, somewhat akin to a favourite aunt some of us are lucky to have. Surrounded by natural beauty, including a river with a waterfall, she symbolizes life's flow and pools of opportunity to be explored. She represents more than just survival; she is tarot's way of promising a thriving life of rebirth and creativity. The huge orange bolster supporting her posture is a sign of positive change that is going to happen, even if the seeker does not apply their energies into the situation. The scenario is one of universal change within the context of what the seeker is asking, and is sending the message that the enquirer should be prepared for a change in their circumstances due to probable expansions of energies. Life is moving forward at a healthy pace; this could mean the seeker needs to update their skills, or perhaps learn something new. The seeker may not have an immediate goal in mind, however this is the time for introspection and broadening horizons. This could be time for reinvention for the seeker, and the introduction of new opportunities.

The Emperor holds the ankh in his right hand and an orb, or globe, in the other hand. The ankh is a symbol of the river Nile and its delta: the river of life. Four rams' heads can be seen carved into the throne, representing decisiveness and power, and as a reminder that the word "throne" is Old English for "three in one." When the seeker draws this card, they are being advised that they have the power to make the decisions; if not the seeker, it may well be someone they are dealing with. The ankh is a reminder to look at past experiences, and the orb symbolizes the future world of the seeker if they make the right choices. Today we live with yesterday's choices. His throne of wisdom is solid and durable, and behind the throne is orange, the energy of change, which is coming whether the enquirer acts upon the information or decides to do nothing. The decision has been made by the emperor and his court to move ahead; if it was a yes or no proposition, the answer is yes. Depending upon the placement of the card in the reading, the time frame possibilities are four weeks or four months. The Emperor in a spread denotes large changes based upon the decisions of the seeker.

The Hierophant is a guardian of esoteric principles and divine knowledge; he is also a mentor and teacher, such as a rabbi or priest. The Hierophant belongs to conservative establishments that expect conformity from their followers. The seeker may want to become such a figure, or perhaps it is a current trait in their personality. This card may be in the spread if the seeker desires to establish a following of their ideals. There are two keys shown in the scene; they may represent truth and healing according to certain principles of the seeker. The Hierophant's right hand is signaling a blessing, which can also be seen in the Ten of Swords. The two monks represent followers of the same beliefs and ideals. Even though this is a spiritual card, it can mean the beginning of a society or movement, political or otherwise. The sceptre is similar to the ankh in representing body, mind, and spirit. Spirituality is not set apart from earthly matters, on many occasions it can be the absolute base of many ventures. This card gives the seeker the blessing to move forward to goals of their choice.

The Lovers declares that the seeker has to allow themself to be vulnerable in order to be successful in this particular venture. This is the obvious card for would-be lovers. The other perspective is that it represents the masculine and feminine components of the seeker. The magnolia tree behind the male figure signifies beauty, perseverance, and nobility. Behind the female figure is a fruit tree bearing food, beauty, and, due to the snake, healing. Both are the same height, symbolizing equality. The garlanded angel with wings is there for protection and spiritual love. Her wings represent immediate flight, i.e. action. The green terra firma indicates growth and easy passage. Crowning the card is the radiance of yellow energy, evenly sectioned, meaning perhaps an orderly transaction. The red mountain in the background resonates with the climax of a relationship or some form of earthly agreement. All in all, this is a partnership card. Whatever is on the mind of the seeker, tarot is signalling that the answer is in love, trust, truth, and honesty, resulting in sustenance, beauty, growth, and healing.

The Chariot is a card showing when to be in control, and when to let go and look and listen to other people. The kingly driver is obviously in command of the chariot, but notice his hands: there are no reins to control the male and female phoenix, representing positive and negative energies. The middle energy would be the state of neutral; when in this state our minds and hearts are open to various opinions, so that wiser choices can be attained. Also, his right hand (the past) holds the sceptre, and his left hand (the future) is ready to receive all newcomers of all realms. The royal city in the background behind the fortress wall is well maintained with its grey walls and red roofs.

The chariot has crossed the river, which may indicate an upcoming journey, while the homestead is in good order. Tarot is telling the seeker that now is the time powerful energies are at hand and in the seeker's favour. The crouching phoenixes show power and readiness to leap forward: Everything is in order, it is time for transcendence.

Strength is a card that covers body, mind, and spirit. When the seeker draws this card, it conveys the message that they are in a state of power and can be in a leadership situation if they wish. The other side of this very positive coin, of course, is its exact opposite, which is to be overbearing, autocratic, bossy, and pigheaded: The attitude that sometimes accompanies strength is narcissism and a closed mind. Tarot is messaging to the seeker to use strength wisely, and allow others to have their own space and time to talk. Even with strength, mistakes can be made and the time will come when support is needed from others to help the seeker through some unknown impediment or problematic situation. Note the logo of infinity above the figure's head, a portent of stability and success within the foreseeable future. One of strength's great partners is diplomacy; they are great assets in interpersonal relationships. This card shows the seeker has deep responsibilities, because it may put them into the position of a community leader. If the seeker has doubts about the question on their mind, this card erases it.

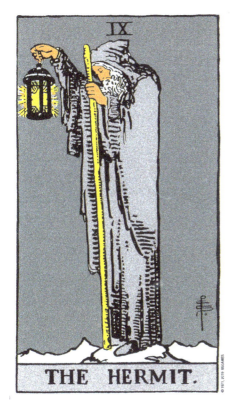

THE HERMIT.

The Hermit: the question is, is he exiting or entering the hermitage? It all depends on what the seeker has in mind. As the hermit is looking towards the left, the usual answer is that he is leaving the hermitage and looking forward. If the seeker is overtired and stressed, he could be entering the hermitage in the future for healing. Either way, tarot's message is rest and revitalization. The light is shining on a new idea or relationship. The figure is garbed entirely in grey, the energy of wisdom; his staff and lantern are lit in golden yellow, the intellectual energy. Tarot is telling the enquirer that wisdom is the main message that will help in their endeavour; if the seeker doubts their personal wisdom, then seeking it from elsewhere is the answer to the problem. This can be done with a three-card reading. What happens if I stay? What happens if I leave? These are two separate questions. This example shows how to ask a definitive question as opposed to just one question (e.g., Shall I stay or leave?). The Hermit also means to use intuition and reflection. This is one of the most spiritual cards in the Major Arcana.

WHEEL ᴏϝ FORTUNE.

Wheel of Fortune indicates improvements are on the way for the seeker through self-education (all four figures are reading books). In addition, tarot is forecasting change, whether the enquirer participates in this universal energy or decides to do nothing. The female sphinx crouches with her sword over her left shoulder, signalling a renewed thinking strategy. The snake is alert to strike if healing is needed. The devilish figure represents caution and prudence; sometimes success does not arrive via a straight line. The angel, the phoenix, the bull, and the lion are all powerful figures of good leadership. All four are resting on clouds of grey, the energy of wisdom. The seeker not only brings wisdom into the scenario, but also gains wisdom from the elevated experience of this particular success story. This exciting energy covers all aspects of the querent's life at this time. Everything in the world is connected, nothing is in isolation; therefore the seeker should stay aware when the change arrives and realize those within his sphere of activities will also be affected. Most changes become involved in compromise.

Justice in tarot readings covers personal and legal visions of balance and equality. The judge holds the sword in his right hand (the past) and scales in his left hand (the future), signaling that the thoughts and actions of the past relate to present and future actions. Legal justice, as many have experienced, sometimes ignores fairness. The seeker is being shown from the reading to look at the full picture of what they are considering and to not look greedily through a narrow lens. Before making a commitment to any cause, the enquirer would be wise to ask if they can execute responsibilities fairly. Time is a precious commodity, as is money; balancing both is the problem for all seekers. If relationships are in question, the same equation is in play. To be too heavy in one area and too light in another probably leads to ill health on all levels. When areas of unbalance start to appear, it follows that something will break down, as with the automobiles we drive, which will not perform well on the road of life if they are not maintained. Truth and healing do not arrive easily, they need nurturing.

The Hanged Man in tarot epitomizes the art of looking from a different angle. Part of the artistic beauty of this card is that when the seeker looks at the card upside down, they notice the figure is unconstrained, as though in yoga pose or dancing. His head is encircled with a glorious halo of shining yellow. Tarot is showing the seeker that a different point of view brings dividends; taking a unique stance will always lead to improved thinking, feeling, and acting. The grey background of wisdom will lead to the orange bough of improved changes. Whatever is on the mind of the seeker, tarot is advising a second look be considered, as it will reveal otherwise unknown facts or new possibilities. Scanning possibilities whilst relaxed will lead to clarity and lucidity, but going to a deeper state of mind through meditation will lift the veil of any mysteries to be discovered. The seeker who draws this card needs to read the small print in any documents or personal matters within the sphere of current activities. Good results are based upon serious investigations.

Death is a card of transcendence, renewal, and the death of old ways or coping mechanisms that no longer work for the seeker. This is a definite black or white situation; it needs commitment and a deep desire for change. If the seeker is leading a life of quiet desperation, then this card is the saviour to take them from just coping to thriving. The art in this card is to draw the attention of the reader and the enquirer to the serious consequences of lethargy and procrastination. If the seeker wants a yes or no answer, this is an obvious yes. Notice the small ship with sails in full wind heading towards the new life. The two children signify two possibilities at hand; the religious figure greeting the seeker is the spiritual energy that awaits the traveller of life. The Death card is also an omen for anyone who is contemplating returning to school or seeking additional knowledge to further their dreams of a better life. The great waterfall represents new rivers and tributaries to be discovered; therefore, be aware of possible geographical transfers that may be included. This white mount will carry the seeker to a happier being.

Temperance shows balance, unity, and good orderly direction, along with patience. The angel figure is pouring water from one cup to the other without spillage, indicating calmness and focus. The pyramid shape on the tunic is transcendence, and the two yellow irises amongst the reeds metaphysically are the bridges between heaven and earth, their colour signifies intellectual acumen. One foot of the angel on land, the other testing the water is the sign of caution. The orange path leading to splendour atop the blue mountains is a journey of educated change that the seeker needs to take for greater understanding, allowing new attitudes of people and events within their sphere. The great span of the angel's wings indicates strength, and possibly far travels in the future. These journeys could be geographical or internal. The water between the two cups of emotion can be interpreted artistically as the ebb and flow of the energy surrounding the seeker. Tarot is advising the enquirer that everything is in order to move forward with caution.

The Devil card is offering the seeker choices. The naked figures represent the masculine and feminine of the enquirer; both are naked and vulnerable, looking for a way out of these devilish traps. Masculinity is the sign of action; look at the devil's torch tending to the tale of the man, indicating that the seeker may be thinking of doing something sinful, or has already acted upon it. Keep in mind that the word "sin" is an Old English term for "missing the mark," therefore it can be corrected through the feminine side of creativity: Her tale is flourishing with new growth and sustenance. The reader should note that both chains circling the necks are loose and can be removed easily, just by both figures choosing to do so. The predicament may have been caused by outside influences, but the seeker's coping mechanism was unable to prevent the outcome. Tarot is messaging to the querent to stop current actions and employ their intuition and creativity for a new future, and to admit to themselves their complicity in the situation, either by action or silent assent. This card is a reminder that we can all do better.

The Tower shows energies erupting, with the masculine and feminine components of the seeker plunging into the unknown; however, tarot has their eyes open and hands outstretched as if the seeker knew something was amiss and had an intuitive sense that something was going to happen, but not where and when. This energy is nature making a correction, showing that the seeker is a little off course. The crown of glory being blown off the watchtower indicates the situation has come to an end, and now is the time to choose a new path forward. When these eruptions occur, whether or not the seeker knew in advance or was oblivious of the dangers, tarot is showing that one side of the seeker's coping mechanisms, awareness, needs to be nurtured, and not to accept certain situations at face value. Due diligence and contemplating the next step are two contributors to awareness that will always serve the seeker well in the future. The three windows in the watchtower, body, mind, and spirit, were left unattended.

> The flame makes the invisible visible.
> — The Kabala

The Star glories in creativity, good luck, diligence, and accomplishments. The huge gold star signifies well-earned recognition. The figure stands for the naked truth, and the water flowing from jug to jug through the figure is the cleansing action of healing. The seven white stars are also signs of healing. The figure with one knee on the ground and the foot on the water, not in the water, signifies small miracles are at hand, such as right time, right place, and right qualifications. The bird about to take flight indicates the time is now to fly forth. The spreading circle of pond water stands for spreading influence within the sphere of the seeker. Water is also trickling from the pond, creating small tributaries to other areas. There are no clouds in the sky, and visibility is good and clear; across from the green meadow are the purple spiritual mountains, to acknowledge all three required components of success: body, mind, and spirit. This card represents the age of Aquarius. A new phase for the seeker is at hand to improve their life situation.

The Moon shines on the emotions of the seeker. The two watchtowers are more than one way of looking at the current scene. The tame dog represents the trained mind, and the wild dog is the instincts, or intuitiveness, of the seeker. The crustacean emerging from the water is the accumulated experience of the enquirer, which is needed to navigate the yellow path towards the Blue Mountains. The yellow leaves sprinkling from the moon are blessings from the universe, in appreciation of the seeker using logic and intuitiveness to process their mindfulness in exploring the cause and effect of actions that may be taken within the context of what is on the mind of the seeker. Tarot is pointing out that what is thought and what is felt are siblings, and both should be considered in whatever decision is selected. Notice that the path is winding and the moon rays are straight, which indicates thinking clearly about what the favoured goal is and being prepared for deviations on the road to achievement. Patience and fortitude are required in this quest.

THE SUN.

The Sun is radiant with promise, light, rebirth of beauty, and positive changes. The small child, girl or boy, is the portent of something fresh and new. The orange banner is announcing big changes, but only if the seeker acts upon all this positive energy; procrastination is the enemy within this situation. The grey horse is wisdom, known as "horse sense," which contains strength and stamina. Behind is a grey wall built over the lifetime of the seeker, holding back any dangers from entering this garden full of opportunities. Sunflowers in full bloom denote the height of summer, a time to reap benefits of past work. The benevolent face of the sun has straight rays (direct energy) and the energy of the universe is shown with the soft curves of indirect waves, putting the seeker on the right wavelength for success within the context of the question. The flower garland worn on the child is a reminder to enjoy the moment, and let go of any thoughts of trying to control the situation. All positive energies are synchronized and tuned for harmony in this beautiful scenario. All is well.

Judgment is upon the seeker; tarot is advising the enquirer to take personal inventory of their behaviour, goals, and needs, and the current situation. It may also be time to make a judgment on another person or group of people. This is the time for naked honesty; it can be a turning point within the context of the question, and a decision is needed. In the cold light of day, everything will become clear, and the trumpet of truth is calling for evaluations of the present, enquiries about the future, and evaluations of past decisions. The naked figures are pleading for guidance; this is the way tarot shows that sometimes the seeker has to ask for help. Not knowing is not a weakness, it's a thirst for truth and healing. Help is at hand through the metaphysical, which incorporates the intuitiveness of the seeker. The red cross on the banner is the sign of healing at all levels. The angel wings are a sign that it is time to fly; with a clean break from old coping mechanisms that no longer perform well, the seeker can do so much better. Tarot says, "Take a fresh look."

The World with the central dancing figure represents balance and harmony. The wreath of laurel is an award for accomplishment. The number XXI (twenty-one) stands for maturity. The four figures: the man is for action, the eagle is for scanning from above, the bull is for power, and the lion is for leadership. Take note of the eagle, surrounded in white; this is for clarity, protection, and healing. Three other clouds represent wisdom. Tarot is informing the seeker to use "eagle eyes" for scanning the entire picture from afar. The red ribbons are for universal energy and actions to be taken by the seeker. The World card pictures great changes afoot for the enquirer: A brand new world is available due to the maturity of number twenty-one, which when divided by three (body, mind, and spirit) equals seven, the number of healing. It all adds up to one of the best Major Arcana cards to be selected within a reading. All depends upon the seeker taking action, no matter how small or large the step may be. Personal and universal energies are aligned.

Minor Arcana Cards

Swords

King

Queen

Knight

Page

Ace

2 of Swords to 10 of Swords

Wands

King

Queen

Knight

Page

Ace

2 of Wands to 10 of Wands

Pentacles

King

Queen

Knight

Page

Ace

2 of Pentacles to 10 of Pentacles

Cups

King

Queen

Knight

Page

Ace

2 of Cups to 10 of Cups

Total of 56 Minor Arcana Cards

King of Swords represents how one thinks and makes decisions. The king is the final decision-maker in the court. When the querent receives this card in a spread, tarot is telling them it is they who have the power to make the final choice. If their decision is to not make that choice, then the energies will continue along the current path, and so the cause of their discontent will be unchanged. Remaining silent is giving tacit assent for the circumstances to continue without any improvement, and possibly to worsen. The king is holding the sword in his right hand. (In tarot, the right is the past and the left is the future.) Therefore the seeker's thinking is a coping mechanism from the past, which may not be working for them anymore. The two birds flying on the left of the card represent two meanings, depending upon the reading and the reader's intuition. It could be a choice of two options, or a solution that has parallel paths.

The king is enthroned upon a granite seat of power and strength. His feet are planted on bedrock of greenery and stone, representing a firm footing which enables the energies of healing and change. There are very few clouds dispersed throughout the skies of blue. His crown is yellow, which equates to an intellectual answer that has to be well researched and studied—which entails reading the fine print in any document or agreement. The difference between experience and due diligence is not having read the fine print . . .

All in all, the King of Swords is telling the seeker that "the buck stops here."

The Queen of Swords represents the contemplation of a problem or situation. She is thinking things over, using the knowledge at hand, which is represented by the one and only flying bird. Her Majesty is facing to the right to review past experiences and decisions. The sword held in her right hand indicates that the past cannot be changed, only learned from. Her left palm is opened to invite further input and valuations from those who are involved, indicating that there are more energies still to discover—more pertinent information is yet to be uncovered, shown here as obscured by the cumulus cloud on the horizon.

This card is telling the querent to be patient, and that eventually what they need to know will come to them unimpeded. Her throne is supported with the intellectual energy of yellow. Depending on the sequence of cards in the reading, if perhaps the following card is the Page of Swords, then perhaps the needed data is to be found in print, as in a page of a book.

All in all, the Queen of Swords indicates that good news is available through memory or further investigations by the seeker. The problem is surmountable through patience and additional enquiries.

Knight of Swords is a member of the court cards, the others are the King, Queen, and Page. All court cards represent "inside information," which can be the information within the seeker, or from a group connected to the situation. The Knight, in addition to being a warrior, is also a hospitaller. On occasion, this card may incorporate stubbornness, shown by the outstretched legs of the horse, its eyes staring back at the rider with a look that says, "Oh! Not again." The knight is charging against the wind, as in going against the surrounding energy. Stubbornness can be a negative or positive force, so the card is reminding the querent to double check the goal and the reason for using such ferocious energy.

People may spend their whole lives climbing the ladder of success only to find, once they reach the top, that the ladder is leaning against the wrong wall.
— Thomas Merton

The Page of Swords brings information to the Court, or perhaps relays information from the Court. The scenery shows the weather is quite stormy, so the energy within the situation is unsettled at the moment. Perhaps change is in the wind. It is also telling the seeker to clear the air, to be honest with themselves and with anyone connected to the question asked. The page is also wondering if all the required information is at hand. The flock of birds above the clouds resembles a sign used by Christians, that of a fish. They are heading to the left, the future, so there is something in the wind that cannot be stopped: Change is in the air. Christianity being pictured here (or any religion for that matter) means deep beliefs are involved in this puzzle. The flock indicates a universal truth to the seeker, as in the adage "birds of a feather flock together," indicating that the querent has come into touch with people of common cause. As the birds are in flight formation, the card may indicate distribution of some sort, whether of intellectual property or merchandise.

The Ace of Swords is a card of triumph. Just as in a game of cards, the ace is a winner. The crown atop the sword is a sign of royal assent. The laurel branch is an offer of peace. The laurel branch is an award for accomplishments. The sword is held in the right hand of God, a promise of divine intervention if needed. His hand is thrust through the clouds of doubt, bringing the seeker into a positive state. There are six blessings of intellectual power floating earthwards. The symbolism of number six is completeness, beauty, high ideals, caring, and motherhood; the six blessings are omens of better times in the offing.

The blue hills represent teaching, learning, and calmness. The magenta hills are symbols of active spirituality. Grey, the major energy of the card, depicts wisdom. The glorious glow emitting from the hand shows clarity, protection, and healing.

Revealing Truth and Healing for personal reconciliation is possible
when reading Tarot.
—Bryan Cavan Doyle

The Two of Swords is a card indicating a state of indecision, or an unwillingness to look at reality; it lives in a world of false hope and aversion to change. As Albert Einstein said, "Nothing happens until something moves." The waters are calm and the horizon is clear in the Two of Swords. So why is the woman refusing to look at what is happening? We can assume the confusion is within. The first move to be made is for the woman to lay down one of the swords and remove her blindfold. She is on the defensive against her inner demons. The seeker is using the coping mechanism of hoping everything will miraculously go away. Another meaning could be that it is someone other than the querent who is undecided. In some religious beliefs, the crescent moon represents a new birth, and cradling it to maturity, which could mean the seeker is really not ready for this change and would be advised to let it pass and await another opportunity, which indeed will happen. This is somewhat akin to pressing the "pause button" and waiting for reality to sink into the psyche of the seeker. Sometimes in the learning curve of life it may be valuable to not do anything and stay where you are. The Two of Swords is not a card depicting weakness, it is a card of caution and reflection. What does the seeker have to gain or lose? The woman's feet are securely planted in wisdom, and her shoes are the intellectual energy of yellow. More than likely, the reading includes an urge to use caution, clear thinking, and sober consideration of the situation.

The Three of Swords card, at first glance, is the final strike to the heart of no return to your norm. This is the moment to realize that tarot card reading is all about truth and healing. It is indeed the death of something in the life of the seeker, whether it be emotional or monetary or spiritual or concerning matters of the heart. All will be well, though, because this is a correction on the learning curve of the seeker. The change may come via outside influences, such as a market change, or a truth revealed about someone or something that is close to the heart of the querent. It is fortunate that the card number is III (three), as in body, mind, and spirit; therefore, this card indicates a healing deep in the soul of the seeker. Nothing is forever; life travels in seasons, plateaus, and circles. Most likely the seeker is nominally aware of the situation and knew that something was afoot, something interrupting their circle. The swords display a blue hue, the energy of teaching, learning, and calmness. The turmoil this card exposes will be conquered with the wisdom the seeker has learned from similar events, either from personal experience or from a mentor's teachings. It is a good time to seek advice from a trusted source. All is well.

The Four of Swords indicates interesting times ahead. The seeker can expect an adventure into new territory, a new way of thinking. Doing away with outdated ways of thinking is key: Notice the entombed sword, it represents the seeker's old way of thinking and previous ways of coping with puzzling events. His hands are in a state of prayer, which shows that the querent cannot solve the problem alone, and must also work on getting in touch with himself. Our behaviour is always preceded by our thoughts. The thought process is the kick-start to our successes and failures. The church window reminds us there is a higher power available to everyone. The remaining three swords are self-evident, being of body, mind, and spirit—all at the disposal of the seeker to use to refill their emptied vessel of knowledge and to give themselves over to a different thinking process, which will be the gateway to needed new solutions. Death of the old ways unburdens the seeker of doubt and confusion, and after a time of rest and contemplation, the missing answer is uncovered. One of the secrets to success is to empty the mind of everything you know and everything you don't know. The seeker has had body, mind, and spirit renewed. They will view the question through a different lens, bringing clarity and lucidity to the forefront of the problem.

The Five of Swords depicts three men, so there is lots of action in this card. Turmoil is in the air, seen in the dramatic cloud formation and the windswept hair of the conqueror, who has retained three of his swords in addition to gaining two swords left by the vanquished. Triumphant in his stance, the winner has a grin of satisfaction upon his face. The two men in retreat are making their way to the water; the victor has not killed them, and so there still is time for compromise. He has not burned the bridges behind him. He has won the battle, but the war is still to be resolved. The card is telling the seeker that, against all odds, they are on the right path. Now it depends upon how much energy is needed to continue on the same path, or whether it is best to re-evaluate the situation and choose another way to go. All Sword cards in tarot are indicators of critical thinking and of determining which road to follow, or perhaps the consideration to blaze another trail. Swords bring to the forefront that it is time to change for the better, and a choice has to be made by the seeker. It shows that this is an opportune time to clarify the chaos and create good and orderly progress to a better life. His green tunic exemplifies healing, the red shirt stands for action, and the orange boots mean change is afoot. Good times are ahead through due diligence and nose to the grindstone.

The Six of Swords is telling the seeker that it is time to make a decision if one has not yet been made. It is time to make a move away from stormy waters where too much energy has been spent simply staying afloat. It's time for the querent to move from the coping mechanism of just surviving into a life of better opportunities that will set free more energy to thrive and grow. The punt is orange, as is the tunic of the man and the garb of the woman, symbolizing the energy of change. The small child is an indicator of a new idea or desire that is looking for a better venue to explore and broaden desires and future goals. The new waters are so smooth that only a flat-bottomed boat like a punt is needed to traverse the new world. The seeker has experienced the difficult path and now has the chance to travel the road more suitable to their talents. All six swords are upright, showing the punter's experience and qualifications to all those he encounters. The horizon is in the calmness of grey, the energy of wisdom. All else in the picture is the blue energy of teaching, learning, and calmness. Whatever stage of life the seeker is in, and whatever realms, whether it be health, wealth, or state of mind, this card signifies a definite improvement in all areas. All shall be well.

The Seven of Swords, with its healing number, indicates a promotion or improvement of current and future energies for the enquirer. The dancing actor with the grinning face shows that his time on the current stage has been fulfilled, and it is time to move on to new horizons. The two swords he is leaving behind are the legacies he has established in the town he is moving from, and notice it is a town of tents, indicating his stay was meant to be temporary. In the background of the scene, a group of people can be seen milling around the campfire at the end of the workday; even their stay is coming to a close. Times and circumstances are in a state of flux. It is time for the seeker to create a new path with the remaining five swords, which are symbols of what has been learned in this particular experience and can be beneficially applied to the next steps upon life's learning curve. The five swords in hand show the seeker is looking for somewhere to place their loyalty; the number five represents Angel 5, which stands for a more permanent situation, whether it be marriage or a more stable occupation, perhaps one which includes a pension and health insurance. Whatever it is, all in all, what is indicated is the need for something long-lasting that includes a reason to meet each day with enthusiasm, one that satisfies body, mind, and spirit. In total, the card is showing that the querent has gone as far as possible in the current situation. And what is needed is space for personal growth.

The Eight of Swords shows self-imposed freedom of movement, due to indecisiveness and an unwillingness to face reality. Change is coming, and the woman does not like it. A female in tarot represents creativity and new production. Therefore the logical equation is that the fear and anxiety is only in the mind, as swords are the symbol of how we are thinking at the moment. Resisting change may be due to a past disappointment that has dragged us into anxiety about the future; we may want to be left alone and not be bothered with anything that is new, because the unknown can fill one with doubt, and doubt is the abattoir of dreams and success. The swords behind the seeker are the thoughts that have brought them to this situation; perhaps they are tired and just want to rest and get away from it all. The one sword that she cannot see is the answer to the puzzle. She only has to wiggle herself free from bondage and remove the blindfold to see the truth, and then the healing will begin. This is when courage is needed to take that one step forward. The word "courage" is rooted in the French word for heart, *le coeur*, so take heart, dear seeker, and move on. Eight of Swords is a temporary stop on the learning curve of knowledge, one that enables us to take inventory of our thoughts and actions.

The Nine of Swords is sending a message: "Oh no, not again!" The seeker is being reminded to not make the same mistake again. Notice the engraving on the side of the bed: a sword duel with a winner and a loser. It is possible the querent is very harsh with themselves when a mistake has been made. Sometimes a perfectionist feels that they are never good enough, and unnecessary recrimination envelopes the querent in the stifling energy of perceived failure and unworthiness. So what is the problem? When such anguish is portrayed, it can indicate a very serious situation such as an addiction to some behaviour or another. There are only ten swords in tarot, and at number nine there is only one option available to tread on the path of success. It will usually mean giving something up. It has come to the point of cease and desist. The enquirer has at last come across the truth, the veil of self-deception has been lifted and the stage is set for the next act. It may be a matter of self-improvement through study and research, or perhaps a life-changing event has been simmering in negative energies and ignored by the seeker. The enquirer has outgrown the current situation and better times are in the offing, but changes are required. It is a good time for the seeker to relax and rejuvenate, even if it is for a short term. A walk in the forest away from the usual distractions would be a splendid choice. The Nine of Swords says, "Take heed, but above all take care of yourself." The needed motto is, "Better and better."

The Ten of Swords is so dramatic it may take your breath away. Tarot likes to demand your attention when the message is important. It is similar to when God sends you a dream that has the solution to your problem. When you do not remember or acknowledge the first, second, or third dream, then you receive the nightmare—to grab your attention. If you still fail to respond to the nightmare, an illness may ensue so you have to stop and listen, and then finally you get the message. Ten of Swords is the nightmare warning. It signals the end of your current behaviours and the beginning of newly learned coping mechanisms. The man's head is facing the river, your new life; beyond the opposing shore are the blue mountains of learning, teaching, and calmness. The yellow sky is your intellectual opportunity, the black void is the new experience to be unveiled. Notice his right hand is in the sign of blessed mysteries, the same sign as in the Hierophant card, which indicates that all will be well when you respond to the constant call of your spirit emitting the truth. In plain English, the card is advising you to listen to your intuition, the sixth sense, or gut feeling that you have been ignoring. The problem may also include a very narrow vision of mind. Tarot is telling the seeker to broaden their horizons and not be limited to self-delusion. As the swords show, the enquirer did not see this coming.

KING of WANDS

King of Wands is holding the blossoming wand in his right hand and looking into the distance with an aura of ethereal energy. The points of reference here are power, decisiveness, and spiritual knowledge. The small humble salamander is on the same footing as the king, and symbolizes the wisdom of the millenniums, trusted truisms many of us overlook due to our very busy lives. The amphibious salamander is capable of regenerating body parts, such as its legs; therefore, it is a reptile of the renewable spirit. The wand represents spiritual or intuitive growth, as its new foliage indicates. Tarot is reminding the enquirer to sharpen their intuitive skills through the veil of the sixth sense, but at the same time not to abandon critical thinking. "As above, so below" is the quote from *The Emerald Tablet* that aptly describes the union of critical thinking and intuition, which can bring correct behaviour for all seekers of truth and healing. The King of Wands card in a tarot spread is a welcome sight for tired eyes, as it can be an awakening to how powerful the querent is in certain situations. It is within their energy to make the right choice at the right time. Timing is so important: One can be too early or too late, but only being on time will get you on the right road to lasting success.

Dare to live the life you dreamed for yourself.
Go forward and make your dreams come true.
— Ralph Waldo Emerson

Queen of Wands is the second court card. The queen is shown holding the spiritual wand in her right hand and, in her left, a sunflower, which is a symbol of growth, sunny times, food (as the seeds can be eaten), and beauty. Note also that on the back drape there is another sunflower, held between two lions that indicate strength and leadership. The cat, who looks somewhat electrified in an alert stance, is a part of Egyptology; cats were revered for attacking venomous snakes in order to protect the pharaoh. In the card, too, are three pyramids—symbols of the transcendence of body, mind, and spirit. On occasion, mummified cats were found in the chamber with the deceased. All of this points to royal assent being given to the plans, thoughts, and desires of the seeker. The queen, being a woman, is in the realm of imagination, where something new is always possible; due to the energy of yellow throughout the scene, this is specially affiliated with any intellectual endeavour.

"My ministers have told me that there is a recession in progress. I have decided not to participate," said Queen Victoria. In addition, with the royal cat protecting the querent and the situation or event in mind, any enemies or impediments will be diminished. Success is at hand when accompanied with patience, due to the sometimes slow pace of court proceedings.

KNIGHT of WANDS

Knight of Wands shows the querent making a presentation to the world. The pictured knight could be either a man or a woman: therefore creativity and action are in union. This knight is dressed for action, and ready for whatever is needed in this particular circumstance, whether it be healing, confrontation, diplomacy, or giving oneself to the service of a worthy cause. The mount is a monument to horsepower and change, and the strength in belief; all in all, it is making a statement: "I'm your man for the job." The ever-present three pyramids show full commitment to the occasion. Because the wand is involved, tarot is informing the seeker that their intuition is most important at this moment of change. The question to ask is: What is it that you really want to do, and what do you really think? This is not change for the sake of change. It is not about something that one is running from, but rather what you are running towards. Tarot is advising the enquirer that now is the time for action in a positive manner. Because the knight is a warrior as well as a healer, it could possibly be a "win, win" outcome to the situation. The seeker has to ask: "What can I lose?" Due to the fact that the mounted knight is facing towards the left, this card is all about the future. Also, they are leaving the desert and heading towards areas of new growth and greater possibilities. It is time to move forward.

The Page of Wands is bringing good news to the seeker as he looks upon the new growth on the wand, which is a sign of expanding horizons, personal growth, and prosperity. The page's garb is entirely in the energy of yellow, symbolizing the seeker's intellect, and orange energy indicates forthcoming changes, which will happen with or without the participation of the enquirer. Notice the emblem of regeneration on his tunic: the salamander. On this card, the three pyramids are very close to the subject, which indicates the change is coming sooner rather than later. His ensemble is that of a dandy who wants to be noticed, which means the seeker really wants to be noticed and appreciated. Even the hat is slightly outrageous in its design. The enquirer may be in a current situation of not being appreciated and has a deep desire to have the opportunity to express their talents in a different venue. The Page of Wands is a card with omens of doors opening for the querent, who need only knock and ask for advice or assistance, then lay their cards on the table and dare to make themselves vulnerable to being questioned about their credentials and experience. The seeker has to let the appropriate community be aware of their desires for self-improvement and to be of greater service to mankind.

Ace of Wands . . . When a seeker of truth and healing selects this card they know that it looks good, but why is that? Everyone knows the ace is a winner. The Ace of Wands is held in the right hand of God, and from it blessings are shaken out to spread and grow. The towered castle in the background suggests stability and power, with its grand view of the surrounding countryside. The hand, emitting a glow of confidence and being thrust from within a cloud of doubt, verifies that energies are synchronized with that of the enquirer. The lush landscape has the energy of healing within the green hills; the yellow energy of the intellect is in the surrounding fields, indicating personal growth; the blue stream winding through the life of the seeker flows with nurturing learning and teaching. With the sacred purple hills in the far background, all adds up to a fortuitous time for the querent. Whatever is on the person's mind when they decided to have this reading, the tarot is showing a positive alignment for this particular search. It would be a shame if the seeker decides not to act upon these omens of a great adventure of improvement in all realms of their personal life. Courage and confidence are needed to fulfill this opportunity. If the querent takes advantage of the chance to make this choice, this could be a long-term game changer.

Two of Wands shows a gentleman holding a globe in his right hand, which indicates he has been harbouring a wish to make a move for quite a while. The two wands are symbols of one of two choices in the offing. He is overlooking the bay, his safe haven, and wondering if he is ready for a trip towards new horizons. The wand on his right side indicates that spiritually he is happy where he resides, but his left hand, holding onto the wand of self-improvement, is tempting him to make steps towards a more fulfilling life; he may feel that something is missing, though he is unsure of what it can be. More information is needed as he looks ahead, towards the future. If he decides to stay where he is, it is pretty predictable how his future will evolve with that commitment. His garb shows that he is doing well financially, so what can be missing? What are the thoughts he has been harbouring? May it be about the actual geographical location in which he resides? Perhaps he wants to change his profession and return to school? This is a time for research and development in a restful place, enabling the seeker to clear his mind of the unwanted debris floating around in this void of limbo, and to balance the choice of potential gains and losses.

A wise man should have money in his head, but not in his heart.
— Jonathan Swift

Three of Wands shows a figure with three wands, the symbols of body, mind, and spirit, with his back facing the reader and seeker, indicating that he has already made up his mind to leave and go forward. Three small ships traverse the river, sailing towards the purple mountains, a destination of spiritual satisfaction and fulfillment. Tarot is suggesting to the enquirer that this is an almost unavoidable journey, one that has to be taken as part of the learning curve of life, that must be completed, even if it is only a temporary event and a return to their regular life is seen as part of the future. Each of the three wands has three budding possibilities, and three by three equals nine, the incubation length of time for birth of a new being. The three ships can be used for commercial enterprise or personal transport, or both. Tarot is indicating that expansion is in the wind, and the seeker must stay alert for possibilities that can enrich their future. The entire picture is one of intuition and of listening to the winds of change. The answer for the enquirer may be found in a book or an educational course, or perhaps from a mentor; of course, the mentor could be either on the other side or here on earth. Tarot is also telling the seeker this is a golden opportunity, as shown in the colour of the card. As the card is a trinity symbol of body, mind, and spirit, it shows that the adventure is in all realms of the seeker's life.

Four of Wands depicts a celebration of accomplishment. Central to the card are the two women raising three bouquets of flowers. The garlands atop the wands are symbols of the community joining the event, as can be seen by the group of dancers below the city gates. Even the entry portal to the town is a garden of flora. Flora is the Roman goddess of flowers, so it is a celebration of beauty and nurturing. The grey walls of the town denote wisdom, and the red roofs show the energy of immediate action. The entire scene has a background of yellow, the energy of the intellect. In addition, the garlands include leaves of green, the energy of healing and abundance.

Tarot is telling the seeker that the time has come for the idea or plan to be put into effect, and efficacy will follow. There are times in our lives when everything seems to be going our way, and yet we hesitate due to fear or perhaps feeling unworthy. This card confirms that the community is on the same wavelength as the enquirer; right time, right place, right idea, as shown by the raising of the three celebratory bouquets. The two women are symbolic of the idea coming to fruition, and what comes next is the actual manifestation; concepts to completion are the bywords of the tarot message to the seeker. To complete this scene of beauty and success, the following quote from Leonard Cohen is apt: "Love is the only engine of survival."

Five of Wands shows five men combatting with wands—is it a war, or just confusion? Depending on the general reading, it can symbolize a robust inner argument within the seeker, or it can be an adversarial outside confrontation of ideas and beliefs of opposing forces. One thing is for sure, conversation is needed in order to uncover the problem and to realign goals with new strategies to achieve success. The enquirer has probably reached a fork in the road and is wanting clarity, or validation as to which path forward to embark upon. Sometimes this card reveals that the querent is caught up in the mechanics of the process and has almost forgotten the actual reason or goal they started out wanting to achieve. Tarot is suggesting a call to truce, to step back and maybe take some time out for rest and recuperation. The word "entropy" encapsulates this situation—"lack of order or predictability, gradual decline into disorder." When we argue within ourselves and with other people, one side of the argument is logical and the other is emotional; no one side can win, therefore we come to a stalemate. Logic and emotion have to be separated from each other to reach truth and healing.

> Order is heaven's first law.
> — Alexander Pope

Six of Wands shows the horseman leading a triumphant parade with his supporters as he holds his wand decorated with the laurel wreath of a winner. The other four wands, carried by his supporters, symbolize the four legs of a table which stand for stability and strength, and carry the possibility of a celebratory banquet to be shared by all within the community. Tarot is advising the seeker that now is the time for action and to let the community be aware of their presence. The grey mount of wisdom, decorated with a blanket of green healing energy, and the rider's boots of orange (the energy of change), along with the red cape of the equestrian (denoting the energy of the moment), all show that now is the time to go forward, with a purposeful meaning of truth, power, and healing. This spiritual card is showing the enquirer that their intuition is synchronized with the needs of others, as well as with their personal dreams of success and accomplishment. The unclouded blue sky gives the impression of a clear vision of the immediate future. There are no impediments in sight to thwart the strategies and goals of the seeker. Tarot is unveiling the confidence needed to be progressive and to cultivate the self-truths within the seeker in order to complete their mission.

Seven of Wands shows six of the seven wands firmly entrenched with the subject, who is grimacing and fiercely standing his ground by either planting his wand or removing his wand from amongst the others. He is showing his opposition to the majority and making sure he is heard and noticed. The question being: Is he joining the six, or removing himself from the majority? Either way he is standing his ground. Tarot is asking the seeker: Are you going to stay, or leave? Being number seven, this card evokes healing, as is also shown by the green energy of healing in his clothing, and covering the ground where he is making his stand. The blue sky shows the energy of learning, teaching, calmness, and patience. The orange energy of change shown on the wands denotes that the change is only going to happen through education and the passage of time. The actual length of time can be calculated by adding up the numbers on the cards and dividing it into the number of cards in the reading, and then through using the reader's intuitive sense to find whether it is days, weeks, or months. Tarot is showing the seeker that it is a matter of choice, not inevitability. When this card is within a reading it usually unveils a deeply held belief of the seeker, or perhaps their adversaries. It could also mean the seeker has deep, controversial emotional and spiritual conflicts. Above all, this card will lead the seeker to a state of healing.

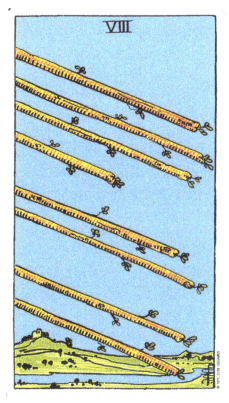

Eight of Wands shows the seeker that they are in a growing state of intuition, as all eight wands are different lengths, or depths of understanding. The enquirer will be pleased to learn that many coincidences will begin to come forth into their vision. It is a time to be in a restful state, as shown through the bucolic scene of the card, with the desirable residence atop the hill, and the meandering river in a state of calm and peace. This stage has arrived after a period of hard work and of attending to details that are, and were, needed to bring clarity into the energies of the seeker. Tarot is telling the enquirer that oncoming days are full of promise if they do the following: listen, read, observe, and sense nuances of small changes. Listen to their body to discern health, read the financial pages for their wealth, observe the everyday news to sense the current energies of their community. In spiritual times like this, attraction rather than promotion brings people and opportunities into the sphere of energy that now surrounds the seeker. The enquirer is in a state of magnetism. Higher awareness is the key to a progressive direction.

There is no such thing as darkness, only the failure to see.
— Malcolm Muggeridge

Nine of Wands shows a tired and wounded figure who has survived tough times and is clinging to his last hope; he has planted and nourished the eight wands behind him and is ready to plant the last wand to complete the garden of a dream he has, and then to wait for the bloom of success to arrive. The hard work is over; from now on it is just a matter of maintaining his creative energies to bring his body of work to completion. His work boots are as green as the thriving hills behind his garden, emitting the energy of healing and material success he so richly deserves. He has learned from his previous errors and is looking forward to increases in his credit accounts on all levels of his being. The figure being alone in this card indicates that everything has been achieved without much help or moral support. There are only ten wands in tarot, so he is really near the finish line. Due to his exhaustion and low energy levels, he needs to rest and get a second wind, and also should consider asking for assistance in the future. Working alone sometimes limits your vision, and you only react to your own applause. An editor and mentor will only add to your success, even when the critique hurts your personal pride. Pride sometimes throws a foggy blanket over the original prize that was envisioned, and you lose your way.

Ten of Wands depicts a sturdy, strong man embracing the full amount of the ten wands and carrying the harvest to town; the bunched wands are in the shape of a "V," denoting victory. In addition to tarot, there is the art of interpreting dreams, and if a wand of any kind appears in one's dream, it is a signal that the dreamer plays an important role in the lives of others and is also important in current situations. For the seeker, this could mean they have a habit of underestimating their role in life. Whatever the enquirer is asking, this card carries the message that they are more than up to the challenge. This card exudes confidence, and is advising the seeker to go to the front of the stage and take a bow. In a reading that involves business ideas, this card is giving the querent the green light to go forward. If it is a matter of relationships, tarot is telling the seeker that this is a long-term contract. If it is a matter of health, tarot is showing that, even if it is really serious, there are medications and treatments available to manage the illness, and a full life will continue. The aforementioned good news stories are all due to the hard work that has been performed previously.

Being prepared for all circumstances is what measures certain victory.

— Sun Tzu

King of Pentacles is a splendid example of making the grade. As a house owner, maybe the king of his castle, the king also alludes to kingship in every level of life, so the card is pointing out to the seeker that if they are not already king, then they are on the path towards their chosen realm. King of Pentacles is a picture of accomplishment, which will be greatly appreciated by the enquirer if they have a goal in mind and are looking for validation. Pentacles are the suit of finance, money, earnings, and investments. The seeker may not have money on their mind as part of the program, however it is the earnings from the effort that tarot is showing the seeker. Money can buy the seeker time, and the other side of the coin, of course, is that they can sell their time for money. The king in this card has arrived at his station through planning, strategies, goals, and patience, not through frivolous gambling. The royal sceptre in the king's right hand has given royal assent to the seeker's ambitions, the results of which are held in his left hand, the winning hand of the future.

> You can only be really accomplished at something you love. Don't make money your goal. Instead, pursue things you love doing, and then do them so well that people can't take their eyes off you.
> — Maya Angelou

QUEEN of PENTACLES

Queen of Pentacles is musing on how her life will change with success at hand and the added responsibilities it entails. The dazzling array of flora in full bloom decorating the card indicates that even though the pentacles emblem symbolizes earthly matters, metaphysical forces are always in play. When you look closely at the colours in the scene, there are a total of seven; by the healing number of seven being included in the equation, tarot shows once again that healing is always front and centre in the tarot philosophy. Part of the message to the seeker is that whatever is on their mind, the queen forecasts great possibilities of success; the next step is to present the findings to the king in order to receive royal assent, which means to write a second draft in order to double check the credits and debits of the situation: Though the initial plan is a sound proposition, going over the facts one more time will reveal the truth. And true to tarot, truth and healing will be the result of whatever the enquirer is looking for. Blue mountains in the background are symbols of a higher moral ground that is attainable. The Queen of Pentacles' attributes are truth, healing, learning, teaching, abundance, action, positive change, and broadening of the seeker's horizons. Change always brings forth the unexpected because all disparate energies are moved into different positions, causing chaos that eventually brings forth a new order, so the seeker should keep in mind that the new road can sometimes be bumpy.

Knight of Pentacles mounted on his workhorse, standing in a fertile field furrowed and ready for planting, indicates a state of readiness to start something new, and shows that profit is plausible. The knight is making a statement to the community that he is prepared to move forward, and now is the time to plant the seeds of new ideas for greater harvests in the future of the seeker's life. Research and development have been completed, and due diligence has been done; all has been examined and double-checked. The pentacle symbolizes the knight's investment into the future. His helmet has a bouquet of edible sprigs decorating the crown, and his visor is lifted away from his face so that he can clearly see what is ahead; this is showing he is here not as a warrior, but as a healer. Tarot is telling the seeker to be honest in their declaration of intent and tell the world of all the hard work that has preceded this moment in time. If the enquirer is seeking employment or a promotion, this card shows the odds are in the applicant's favour. Knight of Pentacles is a harbinger of improved growth and promise of things to be better and better. It is also an accolade of accomplishments and deserved improvements. For the seeker of a better life and improved circumstances, this card is a most welcome sight.

PAGE of PENTACLES.

Page of Pentacles is a messenger of grand news for the seeker, especially if the seeker has ambitions of a more meaningful life. His clothing colours denote the energies of healing, immediacy, abundance, and change. The look on his face indicates pleasure at the future prospects for the seeker. As he stands in a meadow of spring flowers, arable land can be seen below, symbolizing that there is work to be done. The grove of trees is a place of rest away from the heat of the sun, and the mountains of blue, signs of the metaphysical realm, are prominent in the scene. Although it is a pentacle card meaning earthly matters, it is not limited to such earthly limits, and so the seeker should stay aware of their intuition at this time of wonderful opportunities. It is not unusual for successful people to refer to good luck on their path to riches; however, luck—good or bad—is simply a matter of making the right choice. In addition, being able to admit to making the wrong choices is crucial to future success. It is advisable for the enquirer to take stock of past choices and interpret the results in a clear and honest fashion. The current energies are clearly in the seeker's favour, but caution and prudence are not to be forgotten.

Success is not the position where you are standing,
but which direction you are going.
— Oliver Wendell Holmes Jr.

Ace of Pentacles is the card all seekers want to see in the spread when they are in need of direction and validation. Held in the right hand of God, the pentacle or coin radiating white light through the clouds of doubt and indecision indicates a winning situation. The garden in full bloom, with the portal opening to the blue mountains of higher moral and ethical ground, is a seldom-seen opportunity that is available to the enquirer; it is an alchemy of space and time that rarely occurs. The white lilies are the flowers of rebirth, such as seen in the season of Easter in Christian beliefs. The skies of grey are energies of wisdom accumulated through experience and hard work. The ace sets the pace for future activities of excellence and success. The silent enemy of this time and space is complacency due to the smooth sailing in calm waters; what has to be remembered is the journey that brought the seeker to this point, and the people and circumstances that were invaluable in projecting the seeker to this manifestation of stability and security. Tarot is advising to be kind, generous, and grateful. Joy is not always bestowed; it is sometimes earned and shared, therefore multiplied through generosity and respect.

> Gratitude is the most important of all emotions.
> — Hans Selye

Two of Pentacles is a man juggling his way through a tricky or delicate situation, financial or otherwise. It is also about balance of time and funds, though due to the logo of infinity in the exercise, tarot is informing the seeker that there is success in the cards; because the two ships upon the stormy sea are being navigated in expert fashion, they will make it to port. The juggler is standing on solid ground, and his red suit indicates that now is the time to act, even if there are foreseeable impediments. If the seeker is a perfectionist and is waiting for the perfect time, the opportunity will pass by. His orange tunic is the energy of change that is going to happen with or without the seeker's participation. So don't miss the boat. The figure in the card is shod in green shoes, which, along with the green logo of infinity, indicates that healing in all realms and abundance is going to be sustainable for years to come. Even though this is a Minor Arcana card, it has far-reaching and profound life-changing messages that will be realized when the seeker looks back on their life.

Three of Pentacles shows team-work; or, if the seeker is conducting as an independent, then the card is showing what is lacking within the strategies of achieving the desired result. Also, the activity is within an established organization, such as a church or government venue. Number three, as usual, indicates body, mind, and spirit. The rose emblem within the structure sym-bolizes patience for time to arrive in its fullness. Most events have slow and busy seasons, and at this stage the three figures are in consulta-tion about the future: The monk represents the spiritual or intuitive sense of the program, the jester is a reminder that life is not all work and no play, and the craftsman is following the blueprint or plan held in the jester's hands. The craftsman is also in an elevated position, so the card is also about making improvements to the basic plan. Tarot is telling the seeker that whatever they have in mind, now is the time to begin planning, but not to reinvent the wheel; build upon what is already in existence to improve and create the added value to the situation. Also, the goal will be reached by the seeker and appreciated by the pillars of society.

The presence of an active, energetic, successful man, or set of men,
in a place, will permeate the place with positive
vibrations that will stimulate all who abide there.
— William Walker Atkinson

Four of Pentacles has the grey tone of wisdom above and below the figure, and he is facing the reader eye-to-eye with the look of accomplishment, telling the seeker they can do it too. Tarot is reminding the enquirer that they have the experience to make this journey, as the seeker may think everyone has their knowledge. The metropolis behind the successful man is one of an advanced population, therefore the required skill needed for achieving the goal is somewhat technical in nature; even if the question is of relationships, it is something that can be repaired through forthright dialogue. His feet are firmly planted, indicating that this event or situation enjoys the prospect of a long-lasting energy of stability and trustworthiness. If the seeker impatiently wants a yes or a no, it is a yes. However, it is prudent to realize that of the accomplishments shown in this scene, it is patience, perseverance, and paying attention to detail that has brought this man to wearing the crown of success. Four of Pentacles also displays an opportunity for expansion, whether it is for an employee or an entrepreneur. It also demands commitment to the cause, due to the longevity in terms of time and space.

Five of Pentacles, at first sight, shows despair, humiliation, and the feeling of an outcast. However, as always in tarot, it also shows the path to recovery, truth, and healing. When chaos of mind or earthly happenings descend upon us, there is always an exit door near at hand; we need only ask for its location. Of course the answer is always within us, but because of fear and anxiety our world is deep in fog. This card shows the man on crutches with a head wound, and the woman covering herself from the elements. There are two questions for the seeker: 1) What crutches are they using for support? 2) What are they protecting themselves from? To find help in this card, they only need to look above and see the church window, but they are too self-absorbed to notice. If they are religious they will find respite in their faith; if they are without religion, but spiritual, they can employ their Higher Power. The figures are walking towards the right, which in tarot is the past; retracing previous footsteps will only make their lives foggier. Tarot is advising to forgive and move on in a healing mode. Their grief of loss is within the material world, or perhaps their pride has been deflated; both circumstances can be replaced and improved.

Six of Pentacles is a balanced life, with excess funds to share with others. But on closer inspection, you can see the energy flow between the three men: the two kneeling, begging with hands out in a state of accepting, and one standing and dispensing the coins with one hand, and with the scales of justice, or fairness, in the other hand. This card, then, shows the seeker actually could be all three men, distributing the energy from one person to the next in a cyclical fashion. It is a reminder that material wealth ebbs and flows, and that assistance is always at hand and can be reached, metaphysically, through thoughtful meditation and mindfulness. If the seeker's material wealth is ebbing at the time of the reading, then through quietness and solitude the answer will come from within; whether it is by a loan or by re-evaluation of time management, a way will be shown to bring balance to wherever the imbalance may be. This is another case where the trinity of kindness, generosity, and gratitude will realign the energies of the seeker, to bring harmony, truth, and healing back into their everyday lifestyle. This card was created for the seeker who is in a state of abundance, or needs assistance on a temporary basis, such as bridge financing in a business sense, or consulting with a mentor or trusted friend. Either way, it is of a cyclical nature.

Seven of Pentacles shows the figure musing upon his next step after reaping a successful crop from his hard work and diligence. Number seven is the healing number, and the picture shows earthly material healing in action: Now what is the next move? Gamble, conserve, expand, or just relax? This question can only be answered by the seeker, but the seeker wants to know the consequences of his possible actions. This is where tarot exceeds, in helping to recognize the current energies surrounding the enquirer. After the general reading through a ten-card spread, using the Celtic cross method, questions need to be asked through a three-card reading. Possible questions: What happens if I expand? What are the possible consequences if I gamble some of my profits? Will I lose opportunities if I conserve? Shall I go forward on a slow and steady basis? The tarot reader should impress upon the seeker the need to ask the appropriate questions, and for them not to be too general. Seven of Pentacles is such a fortunate card to draw, it would be a shame and disservice to the seeker to not take it seriously. As seen in the picture, colours of all energies are in play, and the promise of a much-improved lifestyle is in the offing.

Eight of Pentacles shows work in progress. If the seeker has not reached this point, then the card is showing that this is the picture of the future: a continuum of work that is sustainable and profitable, made through perseverance, attentiveness, focus, and with vision of good quality and honesty. The work will be well received in the marketplace due to the trustworthiness, as the picture emits, and the thoroughness and quality of the finished product. Notice the road leading from the town to the seeker's workshop; this indicates there is a way of distribution of thoughts and feelings towards the intended goal or desire of the querent. The six pentacles, or coins, hanging on the wall are displaying the seeker's artistry, or accomplishments; the one he is working on represents that there is always work at hand, and the remaining one on the ground shows that the need for their services will always be there. This work in progress could be addressing not only money matters, but also relationship energies and thought processes. Tarot is showing the seeker they have the right qualifications for the upcoming opportunities, and to continue with perseverance and confidence.

Nine of Pentacles, with the woman gowned in rich robes and in the garden of pleasure with her hunting hawk, personifies an individual who has succeeded in her pursuit of personal wealth and earned the comfort of relaxation time and even more opportunities for her future. There are only ten pentacles and she has nine, quite an accomplishment! Depending on what the seeker is looking for, this card has more than one meaning. If it is a yes or no question, then obviously it is yes. The overwhelming yellow energy of the intellect indicates that a lot of thought, research, and development is involved in this particular story; it can be current or in the future. The pet hawk is a symbol of a pet project, and/or scanning further afield and hunting for additional fresh goals. The two trees in the background are there for balance and growth; the surrounding garden in full bloom reminds the seeker that this location is not an arrival base, but something that has to be constantly nurtured to succeed in future seasons: if left unattended, it will ebb into its wild state and all could be lost. Notice the snail unobtrusively crawling from the left corner, a reminder to be patient and also to conserve your accomplishments so you will always have a roof over your head. Success can sometimes bring on addictive habits or activities that poison, and eventually ruin, all that is gained.

Ten of Pentacles shows long lasting stability, and possibly the beginning of a dynasty of some description. Family gatherings, mentored by a grandfather figure, and new beginnings, shown by the small boy reaching out to the pet dog while grandfather is petting the second hound, together symbolize the continuing path of "concept to completion." The reader is advised to be cautious when reading Ten of Pentacles, as this card could also portray the feminine and masculine aspects of the individual seeker, with grandfather as the guru, the boy being a newly born opportunity, and the two dogs as a pair of pet projects. It is wise to remember that the reader's intuition is the main player in this game of reading energies. This card is rich with information in colour energy and symbols, such as in the two banners hanging on the wall, one with the castle and the other with scales of justice. All in all, it is obviously a most positive card, especially with the full ten pentacles on display: Ten out of ten, a most impressive result. Also of note are the parents, looking forward to the future and remembering the past.

KING ♁ CUPS.

King of Cups is in command: Is he the seeker, or someone else? Enthroned, the head of state is seated firmly with confidence, with stormy seas around him almost unnoticed as he gazes into the future. The cup of emotions is held in his right hand—the past—and his left hand holds the future: the royal sceptre, representing the green light for permission to go ahead confidently. This picture is somewhat like the poster created by the British government in 1939, at the start of the Second World War: "Keep Calm and Carry On." Even in times of uncertainty, tarot is telling the seeker the wisest action is to stay emotionally balanced and keep the goal in sight. Behind the throne, a ship in troubling waters is making headway; and on the opposite side is the snake of the sea coming to the rescue, as he represents healing. Storms never last forever, and they are part of life. One can say they are a part of our learning curve. Perseverance is needed in whatever the enquirer is asking about, along with patience, courage, and self-confidence; all of these attributes will take the querent to their desired destination. Expect impediments on the path, everyone meets them at some time or another. All will be well. The seeker holds the truth.

QUEEN of CUPS.

Queen of Cups is regally seated upon her granite throne, emitting strength of focus even though the incoming tide is less than smooth. Tarot is advising the seeker to address their inner strengths and weaknesses. Emotions can sometimes run high and cloud logical thinking. Time out, perhaps a visit to the beach and some fresh air, and taking a deep breath in order to relax and view the situation from different points of view is what is needed. The sea surrounds her but, as always, the tide will ebb and supply more space for the enquirer to move more freely. This feeling of being hemmed in will pass, and there will be more time to think about where to go from here. The three cherubs engraved on the throne symbolize the metaphysical, which the seeker occasionally forgets exists in the heat of the moment. The queen has the look of a person studying a map to figure out which roads to follow to their planned destination. The Queen of Cups was selected by the seeker to show it is time to look at the puzzle and find the missing pieces of the solution, in order to see the full picture.

The question is not what should I do in the future to get it, but rather, what am I presently doing that prevents me from realizing right now.
— Alan Watts

Knight of Cups is making a presentation with his credentials to the community, or to a single individual. This card can represent the seeker or someone they know. The stance of the mount shows this is a formal enquiry, or a serious application to be invited into a particular organization. The courtly knight is a diplomat, a healer, and a mediator or bridge between adversaries. This formal visit has been planned ahead of time and preparations have been, or should be, carefully examined and vetted for a successful outcome. The winding river is calm and welcoming, and shallow enough to be crossed easily into the new territory. Knight of Cups is a card of opportunity, and indicates that this is the right time for the querent to apply their efforts into improving the quality of life. The knight is in full military dress, indicating that this could be a life-changing venture and requires full commitment on behalf of the seeker. Whatever is on the mind of the enquirer, this card is giving the go ahead to move forward and reap the benefits of the work put into the project so far. The future looks good for the seeker, all they need is the courage and confidence to present themselves in public and let everyone know they are in the arena.

Page of Cups is looking at the fruit of the sea in his cup of emotions. Seafood is commonly known as energy for the brain; therefore, tarot is messaging to the seeker that thinking and feeling are siblings, the other two are intuition and action. The page brings the message from the royal court, indicating that whatever the message is, it has been vetted by the establishment of the day. His ornate garb is a signal that this message, announcement, or presentation is ready for public consumption. If this is a yes or no question, the answer is yes. The prince, like the situation, is firmly footed on the ground; the sea in the background appears to be at high tide, which means this is the natural time to launch the idea or plan. The base of the card is yellow, the energy of the intellect, and next is the calming, teaching, and learning energy of blue. The majority of the card is in the state of grey, the energy of wisdom. The total picture shows an abundance of planning, research, and development; if this is not the case, then it should be. All in all, this card is telling the seeker that the message will be well received.

The Ace of Cups. The cup is supported by five water spirits representing the five senses, which mean earthly pleasures brought about by numinous energies. There are some who believe numinous energy is the step prior to enlightenment. Ace of Cups is the messenger of supreme positive energy: though it may not be revealed to the seeker immediately, the seeker knows its arrival like a flash of light into their senses. This insight appears upon a particular action taken by the querent, even unknowingly. Meditation without action is either procrastination or being in a stagnant state of mind where nothing happens, not a ripple on the pond: Are you *nowhere* or nowhere? The dove atop the cup is the sign of peace, the cross signifies balance. The water lilies growing in the pond are emblems of tranquility, peace, hope, and love. Claude Monet's water lily paintings are world famous for beauty and calmness. The water lily was adopted as the national flower of Bangladesh to signal hope and prosperity. This card is a portent of aspiration of achieving the best within one's self and enjoying beauty and pleasure in all earthly forms.

Two of Cups shows an exchange of emotions between the feminine and masculine. If it were not about two people, this would symbolize balance and harmony within the seeker. The winged lion head emits strength and immediacy. The two entwined serpents represent healing on all levels. The bucolic background is a scene of peace of mind and comfortable living. The entire scenario represents compatibility, love, understanding, and mutual interests. If the enquirer is asking about relationships, then this card is screaming out "soulmates." Not only is it an announcement of love, but also of long-lasting friendship. This card can also carry its meaning into business partnerships and collaboration in all sorts of ventures. One of the beauties of the card is the equality of people, ideas, and goals; a true meaning of democracy in action. The querent who draws this card in the reading now has the authority to speak their mind and declare their intentions. This is not the time to be cautious or timid; declare your thoughts and wait for the consequences.

Three of Cups depicts joyous celebrations of accomplishments in the past, present, or future. This card is a validation of the seeker's thoughts and desires on all levels. Sometimes it is a portent of the future based on the enquirer's past failures, or perhaps just poor timing; time has three portions: late, early, or timely. A seeker can be right, but too late or too early. Timing is eighty percent of the equation in success. The three women are dressed in the energies of intellect, wisdom, and action. If expansion is on the seeker's mind, the abundant harvest on the ground signifies that now is the time to act; it is also a sign of the birth of something new. If the seeker is an author, then this is the final draft; the script is now complete and ready for publication. We are all the authors of our own successes; this card renounces failures. The fruits of success surrounding the dancers are energies of change and growth. The blue sky depicts clear vision and temperate weather, a sign of few impediments. The seeker only has to step forward and start walking to their goal.

Four of Cups is a bonus card; three cups in front of the seeker and a fourth thrusting from the clouds in the right hand of God, or higher power, which is the unforeseen bonus. Going into a deeper state of mind, cross-legged under the tree of knowledge, a man on a quest wants answers, as knowledge is the power that leads to the numinous and eventually to enlightenment. Cups are the suit of emotions, yet emotions can lead the seeker in the wrong direction, therefore it is wise not to misconstrue an emotion as wishful thinking. The seeker beneath the tree is training his mind to be in a neutral state, so he can deal with facts and not hurtful feelings. Meditation is a key factor in reading tarot correctly. Through meditation, the reader or enquirer will unveil the next step to take towards their goal. This card is telling the seeker there is a solution to the problem outside of the usual thinking process; intuition or sixth sense now comes into play. Four of Cups is a card to guide the querent through the process that will lead to a successful conclusion.

I don't think it's for them to have an opinion,
because they don't have the facts.
— Maria Sharapova

Five of Cups shows a figure in emotional distress, with three cups upset due to past actions, and two cups standing in reserve and ready for two choices for the seeker to consider. All is not lost; there is refuge and comfort across the river. The question is how to get there. When enquirers take part in a tarot reading, some are in mild shock from disappointing news that they feel sets them back into a void of indecisiveness. Five of Cups is the answer to the puzzle. There are two ways of getting across the river for the cloaked figure: He can wade across if he is impatient, or he can walk along the riverbank and walk across the bridge, because he wants to move forward and resume normality. The reader interprets the choices within the context of the other cards in the set. The knee-jerk emotional reaction would be to plunge into the water, the thoughtful step would be to stroll to the bridge. Taking that stroll will give the character extra time to give the situation more in-depth thought, to extricate him from this mental trap. The bridge is white, the energy of healing and enlightenment, which will help the seeker see more clearly and feel much better. He can leave the three upset cups where they are, this part of his life is over.

Six of Cups shows the need of trust. The two youngsters are symbols of something fresh, something new: an idea, a relationship, an upcoming agreement, or legal document. The exchanging of cups of emotion is heartfelt, though notice the little girl is wearing a protective mitt on her left hand (a symbol of the future), due to some of the flowers also having thorns on their stems. Also notice the security guard is at the end of his shift and leaving the scene. All six cups are upright and the plants therein are flourishing. This card is all about the future and possibly the present. It embraces trust, growth, and success on all levels. The guard is leaving the scene as everything in the foreseeable future is safe and under control. The boy is taller than the girl, indicating that something has already started and that the little girl is a symbol of the future of additional growth. If the seeker is looking for a length of time in this case, it would be akin to a six-year plan. The mitten and the possibility of thorns are reminders of acting with due diligence as the figure has a shadow.

Seven of Cups is looking into the future; the figure's back is towards the reader, indicating that now is the time to move forward. It does not mean to forget the past; once in a while it is worth looking into the rearview mirror to be grateful for lessons learned and to remember past successes. The seven cups of emotional healing run as follows: #1, the head of a man = action; #2, the snake = healing; #3, castle = fortress and home; #4, baubles and beads = frivolous expenditure; #5, laurel wreath = accomplishments; #6, ogre = warding off bad luck; #7, covering future splendour = unforeseen successes as yet. Six of the cups represent the ingredients needed to uncover the surprise in the seventh cup. Tarot is telling the seeker not to take their life too seriously, and at the same time to rid themselves of any self-doubt. Not everything can be under control of the seeker; chances have to be taken within the learning curve of life. However, this card does show promise of success with the appropriate training and attitude of the individual, and with including the art of compromise. Tarot is telling the enquirer now is the time to begin the quest of success.

Eight of Cups is a card of transition. The sun and moon are seen high in the sky together, which means a timeless decision is in the offing: to stay or to go, with the proviso that the seeker has the choice of returning. All eight cups are upright, indicating that the seeker's current state is one of boredom, or that they are in a stagnant situation without the possibility of expansion and with limited opportunities. The enquirer is starting the journey early in the day, with the walking staff in hand because the journey may be long and arduous. Garbed in red, the energy of immediate action, the walker is emotionally equipped for the upcoming quest. The meaning within this card also alludes to an inner journey of self-discovery; perhaps indulging in an educational course to add to their abilities is of benefit, even if it is the beginning of a new hobby that has been playing upon the mind of the seeker. Whatever happens during the journey, it will give added value to their life. Tarot is telling the seeker there is a void within this space and time that has to be filled in order to satisfy their longing. It is time to hit the road of discovery.

Nine of Cups shows a satisfaction of work well done and deserved payment. The figure in the scenario appears to be so happy and content, with his arms folded over his chest and a look of: "I'm here, and loving it." Hopefully everyone who is reading this book has experienced moments like this, and they are quick to come to mind. There are ten cups in the suit, and to have accomplished having nine of them is a wonderful feeling. Tarot is showing the seeker that if they are not at this stage as of yet, it is on its way, and is reached by keeping faith and self-confidence in the daily routine. As usual, there is another side of the coin: complacency, which can be the killer of dreams and the destroyer of success. When in this state of self-congratulations (and sometimes receiving accolades from the community), it is worth considering sharing some of this feeling with others who are in need. Showing graciousness as a winner is the epitome of good manners, and that is always appreciated. The receiver of this card has received validation from tarot.

Ten of Cups is the card of fulfillment. Husband and wife are in touch with each other, the two dancing children and their parents are welcoming the world; this is the perfect card if the question is about relationships. If the question is about a situation other than romantic, then it shows the masculine and feminine within the seeker, along with two goals or ideas than have been planted in the mind and are now ready to be launched into the community. The ten cups aboard the rainbow signify a bridge spanning all required regions of endeavour. The clear skies overlooking the bucolic realm of house and home, within space to work and play, is the dream of many seekers, even if they do not have a clear goal in mind, and tarot is showing them it is still possible to attain if they allow themselves to dream; we all have to start somewhere on the road to accomplishment, all that is needed is an inquisitive mind and a sense of expectancy. Nothing tried, nothing gained. Awake to the world of possibilities, everyone has the right to try, and tarot is telling the seeker the time is now.

The Art of Using Your Intuition to Enter the Energy Field of Tarot Card Reading

The intuitive mind is a sacred gift and the rational mind is
the faithful servant. We have created a society that honours the
servant and has forgotten the gift.
— Albert Einstein

Energy is neutral. Through our thinking we transform the surrounding
environment into a positive or negative situation. In reading tarot, we use
the cards as a point of reference, which enables us to reach the realm of truth
and healing by interpreting the story we see and sense in the pictures thereof.
The enquirer is not interested in what we think, but rather in what we sense.

As we know, matter is made up of invisible molecules that make the matter
into form. These molecules, known as subatomic particles, are rushing around
at great speed and in complete disorder. The job of the tarot reader is to bring
order out of disorder. The first rule of heaven is order. Usually the enquirer
has spent considerable time thinking of the situation in a quest for truth
and healing, with only doubt and confusion resulting. Truth will always lead
to healing, and vice versa. Discovering your personal truth will increase the
healing process psychologically, biologically, mentally, and spiritually. The word
"spirit" has its roots in the Latin word for "breath," or "courage." Without breath
and courage we cannot envision truth and healing, even if we see it. The adage
"seeing is believing" is only true when we add "understanding." Upon entering

the spiritual (intuitive) world, we are able to tread upon the road of truth and healing. Therefore, truth and healing becomes a preventative force, an energy that keeps us in order instead of disorder.

As a point of interest in order brought out of disorder, one only has to look at communities in Japan. The country is always under the threat of earthquakes and tidal waves, yet their gift of art is always succinct and beautifully executed in an order of form and colour. Even the presentation of food is arranged in an orderly fashion. Sense out of nonsense is achieved, so it seems.

By simply asking, "What is it in my current situation that is impeding my progress to where I should be going?" the tarot devotee will always discover another way to make marked improvements in their lives before disruptions and unexpected upheavals occur. As you may have noticed, our lives do not follow a straight path from A to B; this is what makes the challenge of leading a life of beauty and self-fulfillment so intriguing. We must be something of a detective to discover our personal path.

Soul, Spirit, Mind, and Body

Our personal truth is always being broadcast by our soul, and not always heard by our mind and body due to the fact that we are too busy ignoring our spiritual being. As in music, a tune is played by one instrument and echoed by another instrument—this is known as "call and response." Our soul is continuously calling the truth, and to hear it we must be "in the spirit." As in music, this spiritual state brings us into harmony. Remember: Spirit is intuition.

Let us now study how to enter the realm of the spirit. The author will share with you his preferred method; on the other hand, if you already have a proven method that suits your purpose, then by all means continue on your path of success.

To reach a state of relaxation, your brain's electric pulse has to be between seven and fourteen cycles per second, which can be reached with your eyes closed and your body in a relaxed sitting position. The relaxed state is called Alpha; your active state is called Beta, which is twenty-one cycles per second; Theta is the lowest state, six cycles and lower per second entering sleep. On occasion, you may slip into Theta from Alpha; don't fight it, and let it happen because it means you need the rest. To reach Alpha, with eyes closed count in silence from twenty-one to zero; it is very important to count past one and into zero as it represents going into a neutral state of mind, as in giving up personal control and not willing yourself into wishful thinking. Once past zero, pause and silently say, "I am held in the light of The Golden One. I am safe, I am free, I am healing, I am grateful. Thank you."

Stay relaxed for a while, maybe two to four seconds. Open your eyes and begin the tarot reading. Please note that after a few practices of the relaxation method, just touching the tarot cards puts you in the reading state as your body and mind memory will automatically carry you into the relaxed state. On occasion, use the relaxation method to refresh the practice, as it does have a cumulative effect. The same method can be used to send you to sleep, thus healing mind and body, and entering the Theta state. When this happens you may dream more often than you usually do. (Dreaming is a whole other matter of reaching truth and healing, which will be visited in a future book.)

With just a few experiences of using the relaxation method, you may notice the gift of intuition—as described by Albert Einstein—acting in a way of so-called coincidences. As an example, a person's name may enter your mind, and within a short while that same person may contact you, as if by coincidence. This is validation that you are now in a neutral state and in the realm of "call and response."

Now, let us investigate the matter for reading on behalf of other seekers such as you.

How Do You Read Tarot?

TAROT TELLS A STORY

Tarot cards are full of colours, metaphors, and symbolisms that can be interpreted by the reader in so many ways; though when interpreted through the prism of intuition, the focus narrows into the personal truth of the seeker.

An important rule of reading tarot to keep in mind: Under no circumstances is a reading a forecast of future facts, nor is it a prescription that will cure any illnesses or dysfunctions, nor a diagnostic application to any circumstances.

Tarot is a guide to personal truth and universal healing; it is to be used in a respectful, dignified, and confidential manner.

Position yourself in a state of relaxation, take a deep breath, exhale, and relax. Now randomly choose a card from the pack using your weaker hand and place the card face down. Again, take a deep breath and relax. If you are right-handed, use your left hand, and vice versa. Turn the card face up. Ask yourself: "What do I see?" Certain aspects of the picture card will attract your attention. Notice your mood. Empty your mind of everything you know, and then empty your mind of anything you don't know.

Allow a story to enter your psyche. Do not edit. This is your intuition in action, even though it likely won't make any sense to you. (Perhaps it does make sense to someone else.) Free yourself from analytical thinking for just this moment.

At this time, I would like to introduce the reader to the interpretations of energies within colours, as it will help the participant to understand interpretation of tarot in a broader sense.

The first seven colours are within a rainbow and also signify the seven chakras.

1. Red – Energy, as in blood;
2. Orange – Change;
3. Yellow – Intellect;
4. Green – Healing and abundance;
5. Blue – Calming, teaching, learning, and communication;
6. Indigo – Intuition;
7. Violet – Spirituality; (The rainbow is the spiritual bridge between you and your deeper self.)
8. White – Protection and healing;
9. Gold – Some have named gold as the ultimate healer, it is also enriching;
10. Silver – Refining;
11. Brown – Earthly;
12. Black – Balance;
13. Pink – Love;
14. Turquoise – Complex situations.

When reading tarot, colours do not have to influence your interpretation; they only do if you are attracted to them. And it does not have to be the major colour of the card.

1. The energy of colours can add nuance to a reading. Take King of Pentacles as an example: the background energy is yellow, the energy of the intellect, and the king is holding the pentacle in his left hand (the future), therefore the reading may include intellectual properties such as manuscripts, paintings, music that will produce monetary value in the future.
2. Many professionals that the author has had readings from never mentioned energies or colours. Perhaps you are of the same ilk. It is not a matter of being right or wrong; it is a matter of magnetic attraction through the reader's individual intuition.
3. Every story has some colour to it. It does give a more distinct quality to the reading.

Tarot Card Spreads

Choosing which spread to use depends so much on feeling comfortable with your choice. The author's three favourite spreads out of so many choices available are:

Celtic Cross Spread,

Three Card Spread, and

Canada Geese Formation.

Celtic Cross Spread

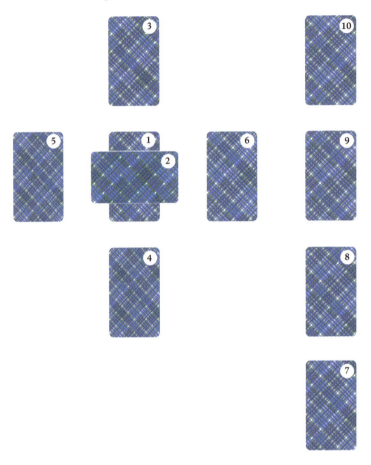

Celtic Cross Spread can be used for general information about personal and surrounding energies. This spread has a total of ten cards, as shown on the ensuing page. The number one card usually illuminates the crux of the matter, whether it is an impediment or a strength of the seeker. On occasion, the seeker may not recognize the value of the card until further into the reading. Cards two through ten tell the journey of the seeker. This particular spread opens the door to possible further enquiries that may have more focus. It is important for the reader to remember that the querent may not have a particular problem in mind. The reading is akin to reading a person's pulse or heartbeat; it is in the form of a general check-up.

After the reading, the seeker may have a pointed question. In this case, the author suggests a Three Card Spread for each question.

Three Card Spread

The Three Card Spread is used for the seeker's questions that have more focus. It is important how the question is framed. As an example, "Will I ever be happy?" is too vague. A succinct question would be "Shall I move from Toronto to San Francisco?" This question has to be broken down into two parts as follows: "What if I stay in Toronto?" and "What if I move to San Francisco?"

Canada Geese Formation

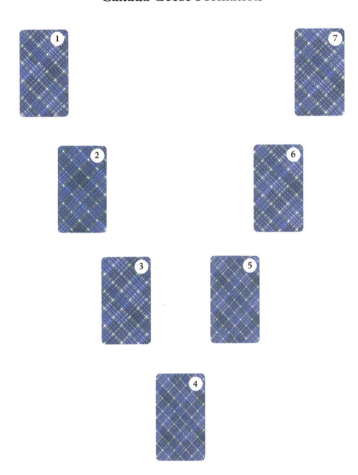

The Canada Goose Formation is used when a decision is needed where a plan is firmly embedded in the seeker's mind. In this case, let us assume the seeker has decided that moving to San Francisco is the favoured choice.

#1 card is past influence; #2 card is present circumstance; #3 card is upcoming influences; #4 card is best course of action; #5 card is the attitude of others; #6 card is possible obstacles; #7 card is final outcome.

In addition, if you are using numerology, number seven is the number of healing. In some cultures, number seven is also the lucky number. And no matter how much planning and research and development is involved in solving a problem, there is always the matter of being lucky.

The dark road
The light road
Our travels through life
Have been on both.

The dark side
Can sometimes
Be a relief
Though usually

Ends in grief.
The light
Can sometimes
Be too bright
It illuminates
Our failures
But also
Makes us
The saviours.

The choice
Comes through despair
Grants us
An opportunity
To repair

From all the wrongs
Our soul erases
And guides us gently
To enlightened places
Of love and peace
And Oh!
Such relief.

A.A Hugget. 2020.

CPSIA information can be obtained
at www.ICGtesting.com
Printed in the USA
LVHW021135260523
748103LV00003B/4